# WISDOM FROM THE NINJA VILLAGE OF THE COLD MOON

by
Stephen K. Hayes

Calligraphy by Kiyomi Fujimoto

Copyright © 1984 by Stephen K. Hayes
All rights reserved

Previously published by Stephen K. Hayes as
Wisdom from the Ninja Village of the Cold Moon
Contemporary Books, Chicago, IL, 1987
ISBN: 978-1-9553428-5-8
Previous ISBN: 0-8092-5383-6

www.StephenKHayes.com

# TABLE OF CONTENTS

ORIGINS OF THE WISDOM ................................. 1

HERITAGE OF THE NINJA ................................. 5

THE ART OF INVISIBILITY ................................. 9

TOOLS OF YOUR INTENTIONS ........................... 17

RIDING THE CYCLES OF NATURE ...................... 29

LOVE .............................................................. 37

VIEWING REALITY ........................................... 43

UNFOLDING OF THE ELEMENTS ....................... 59

HARMONY WITH THE COSMOS .......................... 73

CLOSE OF LIFE ................................................ 81

ADMONITIONS OF THE KNOWING ...................... 85

ABOUT THE AUTHOR ......................................... i

For Rumiko
strength in the shadows
*In* of my *Yo*
ever the true *kunoichi*

# ORIGINS
## OF THE
# WISDOM

Lost in the mists of a thousand years of legendary Japanese history, stories of seekers of spiritual revelations in the mountains overlap tales of warrior rebels striving to reverse military and political defeats in the shifting capitals of ancient Japan. Born of this unique evolution was the coming into being of Japan's secretive warriors of the night - the ninja.

Forged from organic experiences in the haunted mountain peaks and mist shrouded valleys of Japan, blended with the revolutionary teachings of strange and radical methods of warfare, the ninja created a radically different way of life from the ordinary Japanese.

Pilgrim seekers met Taoist sages fleeing warfare and political upheaval in China. Exiled T'ang generals formed underground communities with rebels on the run from the Japanese Emperor's court. From the remote fog-shrouded peaks and marshlands of south central Japan's Iga province to the towering and forbidding ridges of Nagano's Togakure Mountain, hidden collections of shugenja yamabushi seekers in the wilderness explored the limits of human vision and the expanse of esoteric knowledge. Wresting the secrets of eternal power from the souls of the very mountains themselves, the warrior wizards blended the tenets of imported Himalayan scriptures with indigenous ascetic practices. Thus was born a comprehensive system of physical and spiritual survival in the face of overwhelming odds.

But possession of the wisdom brought on the condemnation of the ruling powers. Death was the reward for those caught sharing the mystic teachings of the forbidden secret knowledge. Cruel generals led armies up the mountains to burn down temples, ostensibly for political purposes, but who can question the cultural conflicts that motivated them?

In the mountain wilderness, the mystics sought sanctuary for the life ways handed down to them from their ancestors. Prompted by political and cultural scorn, economic pressure through excessive taxation, and calculated military manipulation, these revolutionaries turned their powers toward survival. They allied themselves with lords of outlying provinces who were sympathetic to their cause. New methods of protective warfare were devised through which the power of the wisdom was harnessed.

Vastly outnumbered and prohibited by law from defending themselves, the once forgotten residents of Iga and Koga transformed their harmonious existence with nature into a radically different approach to self-protection. Subtle, dark means were drafted in contrast to the bold glory of cavalry charges. Suggestion replaced confrontation. Fears of the mind became weapons to overcome even razor sharp swords.

Thus was born the legacy of the ninja. Shadow warriors of the night, invincible strategists who brought the promise of victory on the strength of their intention alone, they took their place in the chronicles of Japanese history.

Wisdom from the Ninja Village of the Cold Moon is the author's imaginative rendering of what could have been part of a scroll inspired by the epic saga of Japan's ninja. Tucked away in rugged mountain forests and lowland marshes, mysterious Iga was home to countless villages of ninja families quietly existing as farming communities. Far from well traveled paths, these ninja villages were training grounds for development of subtle combat and espionage skills, the ability to live in harmony with natural forces, and the effective channeling of the powers of the universal process.

Every clan or family tradition of ninjutsu, the ninja's martial art of stealth and perseverance, possessed its own scroll of ultimate knowledge, the sacred makimono. These cryptic scrolls of wisdom contained the secrets, the revelations, the methods, and the history of the family The holder of the scroll possessed the authority of its teachings and the powerful, silent endorsement of preceding generations of ancestors. Each successive generation added its own insights and signature seals, and passed the scrolls on to the next chosen heir.

Wisdom from the Ninja Village of the Cold Moon offers timely guidance for approaching self-awareness and the comforting realization that the seemingly confusing events of daily life are but mere reflections of the all-pervading order of the universe. The warrior of today may no longer garb himself in chain link armor or carry the sword of his ancestors. But his heart must yet be a source of light. He must yet learn how to steel his intention toward the attainment of that which must be. His method for accomplishment in the contemporary realms of commerce, service, education, and personal relationships today is the timeless "art of winning", the essence of the wisdom from the ninja village of the Cold Moon.

# HERITAGE OF THE NINJA

*Wisdom From the Ninja Village of the Cold Moon*

Like the fathers of your grandfathers
it was your destiny
to become a ninja.

From teachers in far-off lands
your ancestors discovered
the secrets of the universe
and the means
to complete joy in existence.

For this
they were hunted down in their mountain homes
by those who feared
the potential of enlightened common men.
Thus was born the legend of the invisible warriors,
mountain mystics who guided their powers
into ways of protecting the innocents they loved
and the truths they sheltered.

Yours is a legacy of service to those in need,
protection to those in distress,
and strength to those who are overpowered.
Your martial art is the way of stealth,
working your will without action.

Your reward is spiritual growth
and the opportunity to be
a conscious part of the scheme of totality.

You will be misunderstood
for utilizing violence to create authentic peace.

You will be condemned
for using deceit as a demonstration of your bravery.

You will be despised
for employing trickery to allow others to see reality.

You will be seen as an executioner
though you are a priest.

Men will call you coward
though you battle the dragons of fear and ignorance.

Welcome to the family.

# THE
# ART OF
# INVISIBILITY

*Wisdom From the Ninja Village of the Cold Moon*

**N**inja
skills in which we train
would best be known as
*the art of winning.*

The warrior of merit generates victory
in ways that do not cause others to feel defeat.
He wins before the conflict erupts,
succeeds before the challenge appears,
and possesses his prize
   ...before anyone thinks to oppose him.

You will assist the sincere
with your ability to win with the spirit.
Their dream becomes the force of your vision
which becomes a vibrant intention
taking shape in the mind
to be woven into the fabric of history.

We will know that we have won
when we have attained what we needed
and the world is a better place
as a result of it.

**B**ecome one with the small animals of the forest.
Teach them not to fear you.
Move with natural gentleness through the realm
you share with them.
These precious creatures
are your family
and they will help you
when you ask them.

Learn the home of the fox.

Memorize the song of the birds.

Answer the chirp of the cricket.

*Wisdom From the Ninja Village of the Cold Moon*

The benevolent warrior
understands the true scope and priorities
of warfare.

He first defends his community,
the countryside that shelters and feeds him
the neighbors who surround his family.

He next defends his family alone,
the ones who turn to him for deliverance,
the people who share his love.

He lastly defends himself.

In the giving of strength to protect
meaningful places
and loving faces
the warrior serves his own heart.

**D**espite the love you feel
and the joy you radiate,
there are those misguided persons in the world
who would see you harmed.

They will confront you with fists or await you in the darkness
with their blades drawn.

Do not fear them
or become angry with them.

Allow your heart to hold an emptiness of purity.
Your receptive spirit will hear the sadness and rage of your
attackers' intentions
and your body will flow
with the winds of their hatred.
You will take them to the destruction they seek.

And as the dust settles
and the blood dries
do not let your own joy decrease
nor find the world any less beautiful
simply because some persons refuse to see you
with eyes that love.

*Wisdom From the Ninja Village of the Cold Moon*

The ninja trains to hold an empty heart
to lose the singularity of self
and become a part of the scheme of totality
where actions are simply actions
and words
merely words.

Do not hate
   ...and your enemy will not know
   ...that you bring his destruction.
Do not fear
   ...and you will not be controlled.
Do not rejoice
   ...and you will not surrender your mindfulness.
Do not possess with your love
   ...and you will have nothing to lose.
The empty heart is open and able to receive.
Do not allow it to become cluttered
   ...with the chatter of the mind
     ...colored with the way that you want to see things
     ...or twisted to fit the way that you feel things
     ..."ought to be".

This is one way to be invisible.
To simply become a small part of the night
moving with the winds and shadows
doing what must be done
completely void of emotions
so that no one's mind can feel you
no one's heart can hear you.

*The Art Of Invisibility*

From the seasoned veteran of many battles,
learn the secret of permitting your attacker
to create his own defeat.
Use patience, receptivity, and unshakable spirit
to overcome his raw brash strength.
The moment before he flings his weapon
causing you to duck away in defense
he lifts his arms.
Ha! Did you see?
The moment before he lifts his arms
causing you to shift your feet for advantage
he hefts his shoulders.
Ha! Did you see?
The moment before he hefts his shoulders
causing you to move into alignment
he tightens the center of his chest.
Ha! Did you see?
The moment before he tightens his chest
causing you fly into range of his presence
he grasps for his target with the force of his spirit.
Now! Time and space freezes
at the very moment of the birth of his intention.
Push forward your arms
and allow him to fall helplessly onto your weapon.
How coldly simple.
Ah! You did see.

*Wisdom From the Ninja Village of the Cold Moon*

**V**ision!
The *jonin* commander of our family effort,
warrior, wizard, philosopher,
sees the vast and moving picture
from his aloofness.

Organization!
The *chunin* executives
mirror our leader's vision
in pragmatic reality
by accommodating
the procession of heaven and earth.

Action!
The *genin* field agents
working the will of the knowledgeable
bend their skills
to forge destiny
and create what the future will call history.

Success is assured
so long as the whole
is dedicated to the welfare of the parts
and each of the parts
perceives their value
to the whole.

# TOOLS OF YOUR INTENTIONS

## Tools Of Your Intentions

These are to be the tools of your trade,
fashioned under the moon
from patterns that are part of our family heritage.
The steel from the earth
and wood from the forest
are tempered by the fire
and washed in the stream for purity
to become the servants
of the winds of your intention.

Use your weapons with prudence.
Employ them only when
the cosmos demands it.
Use your creativity as the first means
of preventing danger.
When you cannot prevent, avoid.
When you cannot avoid, confuse.
When you cannot confuse, dissuade.
When you cannot dissuade, hurt.
When you cannot hurt, injure.
When you cannot injure, maim.
Only when the scheme of totality demands you be its messenger,
  ...kill.

*Tools Of Your Intentions*

**N**ine throwing stars of steel
pocketed over your heart
carried into the unknown
to stun those who would cut you down.

Like their luminous cousins in the heavens,
small diamond stars sail through night skies
on their own purpose.
Blades born on dark winds
raining from the ninja's hand
to wage a tiny, three-second war
that peace might follow.

*Wisdom From the Ninja Village of the Cold Moon*

Take and grasp this,
your secret short sword
with its humble steel and wrapped handle.
Use it as a probe
as a step to scale a wall
as an underwater breathing tube
as a measuring device
as a source of blinding an attacker in a cloud of dust
as a means for fighting your way out of a tight hallway or room.

The samurai holds his sword to be a thing with a soul.
For you
it is just another tool,
one more implement
to assist you in doing what you must do.

*Tools Of Your Intentions*

**T**he shaggy oak
beneath which you played
as a child on summer afternoons
has yielded you this fighting staff.

Take and apply it against your attackers
with the same resolute stance
as the oak rooted among the rocks.
Imitating the mighty limbs of its source,
the oak staff hums as it flails the winds
and resounds as the skulls of the foolish
strike its hardness in futility.

Is it truly violence
if brutal oppressors happen to stand
where the tip of the oak staff
chooses to sail?

*Tools Of Your Intentions*

The steel extension of your very life force
shoots forth
to entangle the death dealers
who stalk you in the darkness.

Like the separate subtle effects
that become the events
that bring about the war
the long chain weapon rattles out,
one link at a time,
to ensnare the distant enemies
who lurk plotting your humiliation or death.

Whirling above your head before the strike
the cool links' unearthly whine
is sufficient chastisement
for those who willingly chose to go out of their way
to abuse your loved ones
in contemptuous disrespect.

*Wisdom From the Ninja Village of the Cold Moon*

To call the killer
cold-heartedly hacking limbs from torsos
and spraying the green forests red
   ...a swordsman
is like praising
the cleaving butcher in the marketplace
   ...as a surgeon.
The man who would learn blade technique alone
is no better than a woodcutter taking apart a forest.
The ninja would be a swordsman
learning ways of allowing the blade
to follow the scheme of totality.

Forcing the universe
to follow the whims of the blade
is perversity
that can only rebound in tragic repayment
for the arrogant deeds
of the ignorant sword wielder.

*Tools Of Your Intentions*

The dark fabric
of your combat garb
does indeed
permit you to blend with the moon shadows
so that none may know your presence.

More significantly
the dark raiment becomes a special priest's robe
as you depart
on your night endeavor of mercy.
Just as the black tarp
pulls in the warmth of
even the winter sun,
your dark cloak is symbol
of the woe you willingly take on
in defense of the gentle ones
you live to protect.

Your strength
is the boldness
with which you shoulder
the oppression
that would crush
the pawns of the brutal.

# RIDING THE CYCLES OF NATURE

*Wisdom From the Ninja Village of the Cold Moon*

All is growth.
All is change.
Such is the way of all natural substances.

In the unfolding of the pentagram
we reaffirm that
the earth produces the metal,
the metal produces the water,
the water produces the wood,
the wood produces the fire,
and the fire produces the earth.

In the cycle of nature
the law is ultimately
growth
for change.

**A**ll is change.
All is growth.

The pentagram pivoted on its axis
is a chronicle
of the demise of all natural substances.

The earth subdues the water,
the water subdues the fire,
the fire subdues the metal,
the metal subdues the wood,
and the wood subdues the earth.

In the lessons of nature
there is wisdom for the fighter.
The mystical combatant
becomes the whisper of the leaves
the smell of the earth
and the taste of the sea
to live to celebrate
yet another day.

The law of resistance in nature is ultimately
change
for growth.

*Wisdom From the Ninja Village of the Cold Moon*

The earth will overcome the water.

Just as the dam
restrains the flood
and the riverbanks channel the flow
the ninja's patient stability
and firm command of the situation
will outlast and defeat
the scattered energies of the hasty adversary.

The hysterical pour through the front gate
spreading out in wild pursuit
overlooking the intruder who calmly sits among the rocks
in their very own courtyard.

*Riding The Cycles Of Nature*

**T**he water will overcome the fire.

Just as the gentle rain
douses the flaming embers
and the cool towel
eases the fevered brow,
the ninja's cunning
and surprising tactics
will confound and defeat
the impatient fury of the imprudent adversary.

Ripples in the surface of the moat
created by a stone
discretely thrown
are blasted with the arrows
of enraged pursuers
as the ninja scales the wall unhindered.

*Wisdom From the Ninja Village of the Cold Moon*

The fire will overcome the metal.

Just as the searing coals
turn iron nails to glowing soup
the ninja's tenacity will prevail in victory
against logically unfavorable odds,
thwarting the dogmatic enemy
who had overlooked the power of intention.

The tattered survivors
stagger back to the castle
murmuring in bewilderment
telling tales of the one crazy ninja
who routed them all
as they attempted ambush.

*Riding The Cycles Of Nature*

**T**he metal will overcome the wood.

Just as the fine steel teeth
saw through the timber
and the sickle
mows down the reeds,
the ninja's methodical logic
will win out when matched against
the enemy's lack of vision
and reliance on untried assumptions.

The ninja watches wordlessly
as the traitor smiles behind his mask
while buying the lies
that he believes will bring him power
instead of the execution
that secretly awaits him.

*Wisdom From the Ninja Village of the Cold Moon*

The wood will overcome the earth.

Just as the tangled grasses
take over the mountainside
and the roots of the pines
split clusters of boulders,
the ninja's inventiveness and creative outlook
easily defeat the immobilized enemy
trapped in his own morass
of ponderous narrow vision.

Aloft in the branches
the fugitive waits with his brothers the crows
looking down
on the helmets of the seekers
who scan the dust of the path
hunting for tracks.

# LOVE

*Love*

**Ka jo wa raku**

The ninja's heart
is like the wild flowers in the meadow
the true epitome of love.
Flowers live well
happily giving off their colors and fragrances.
They know themselves as neither good nor bad
though we may speak of
"weeds" and "blossoms."
The thistle grows
beside the rose.
The flowers are there for all
never needing to deem the wicked from the just.
They are simply there giving to us
   ...if we choose to behold them.

They know enough to bend in the wind.
They know enough not to bend
when there is no wind.
They grow around any impeding obstacle.
Indeed many are the dreary stone walls
that have been taken over
by the joyous faces of the morning glory.

Flowers are not despondent
when caught in a cold rain
nor are they inordinately ecstatic
on a sun-filled afternoon.

Their joy and sorrow
are the same thing.
They seem to realize patiently

that sunshine and rain,
growth and pain,
are all there as part of the total scheme.
No matter what the circumstances
of the current moment
those circumstances too will pass.

If the flowers are mowed down
they will sprout again
without bitterness or vengeance.
They neither fear nor hate
the ever-coming frosts of winter,
and they know the autumn is always there
behind them
but that knowledge does not make their blossoms
any less bright or plentiful.

Such is the love of the flowers.
Natural harmony
giving only what is theirs to give
accepting all that comes to them
demanding nothing.

Such is the love of the warrior.

*Love*

**S**he is yours now
but you will never possess her.
Hers is a spirit that dances in the world
as does yours.
Hers is a breath that flows with the universe
as does yours.
Her eyes
like yours
see the crows winging across the autumn sky,
see the vast forest stretching beyond our village,
see her loved ones grow old
with the passage of the seasons.
Your heart may leap
with the touch of her hand on your cheek.
Your heart may sing
the songs written by her graceful laughter.
Your heart may own all these experiences
but you will never possess her.
She is her own unique piece of grand eternity
in which there is only the illusion of a past,
only the pretense of a future.
You possess nothing more than this present moment in life.
So share her joy,
feel her love,
and, as the spring winds roll across the marshes
and sunlight ripples across flooded rice fields,
become a part of her story
as she of yours.

*Wisdom From the Ninja Village of the Cold Moon*

It is so easy to confuse our experience or expression of love
with the love itself.

The child's love for his parents
is experienced as **reliance**.

The young man's love for his lady
is experienced as **passion**.

The warrior's love for his country's people
is expressed through **strength**.

The old ones' love for the young
is expressed through their **provision**.

Dependence,
lust,
ignorance,
and possessiveness
are all lesser qualities that easily assume
the disguise of love.

Love is an absolute quality.
This is a little-known secret.
There are no divisions or degrees of love.
It is not possible to love a little more
nor to love a little less.
Love itself is complete.
Love is recognition
and total acceptance.

# VIEWING REALITY

*Viewing Reality*

**P**eople are helpless
only when they see themselves as helpless.

The present is our only opportunity for power.

The passage of time controls
and bends all things
only when we believe in
the passage of time.

The future lived
is merely yet another
Now.

*Wisdom From the Ninja Village of the Cold Moon*

**Om!**

    **Mani**

        eternal cold blue diamond

            (ultimate abstract truth)

                grasped as the experience of

                    **Padma**

                        lush warm red lotus

                            (life's truths experienced)

                                  **Hum!**

The will of the divine ultimate order
propels itself into reality
through embodiment as the dust of the world.

The dust of the world
can only be in extent
as a reflection of some greater ultimate order.

The twin mandalas reveal graphically
two views of the identical universe
that we live and experience
as one single process.

*Viewing Reality*

**K***ongo-kai* diamond realm
vast and timeless extent
of universal truth,
no beginning,
no end,
tale of our own individual life story
as seen stretching between ancient ancestors
and distant progeny,
the god's eye view of actuality.

**T***aizo-kai* matrix realm
immediate moment's realization
of the temporal manifestation of truth
this second, this second, this second,
the glimpse of our own interaction
with all other aspects of the universe
right here in this very fleeting instant,
the being's eye view of reality.

Yes, you can see both inside and outside
with the very same glance
if only you realize the choice.

*Wisdom From the Ninja Village of the Cold Moon*

**A**shuku Nyorai as personification of water!

In the east
we behold the wonder of highest self as
wizard scientist
holder of secrets
wielder of mysteries
one who travels inward to know.

Each of us
in his or her own unique way
wants to be
*right.*

Authenticity
is power, but...
Beware of the corruption that turns cool exploration into cold estrangement and dismissal of others out of fear of loss.

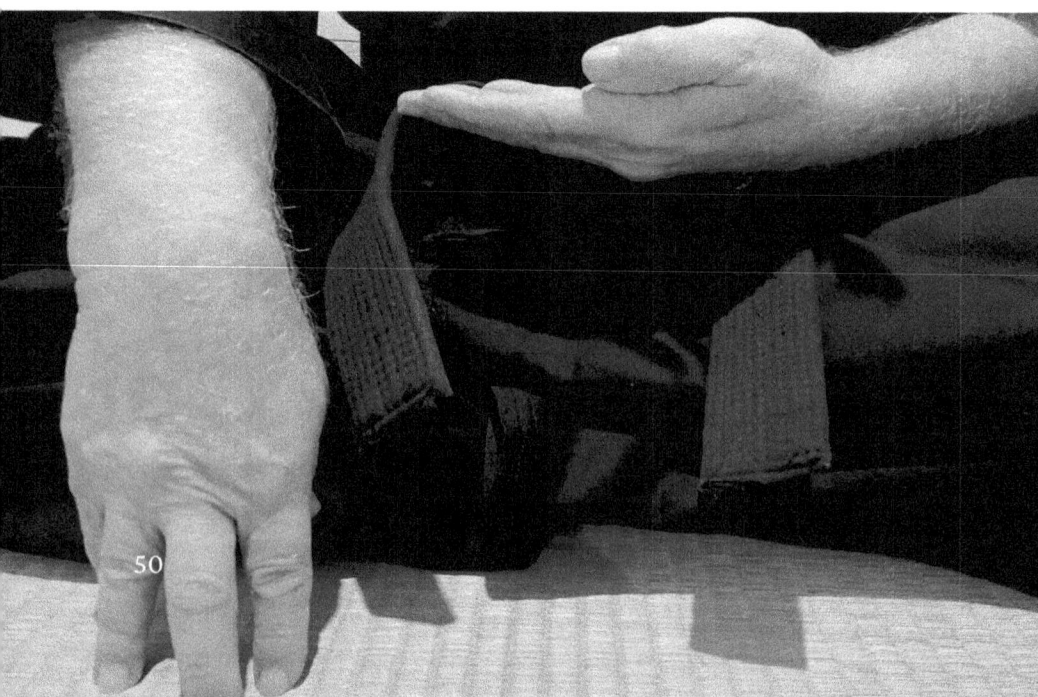

*Viewing Reality*

**H**osho Nyorai as personification of earth!

In the south
we behold majesty of highest self as
noble ruler
the generator of order
the rewarder of merit
the one who inspires all others to greatness.

Each of us
in his or her own unique way
wants to be
creator of his or her own boundaries.
We all long to feel
our *importance*.

Abundance
is strength, but...
Beware of the corruption that turns confident self-assurance into
arrogant narrow-mindedness out of fear of losing control.

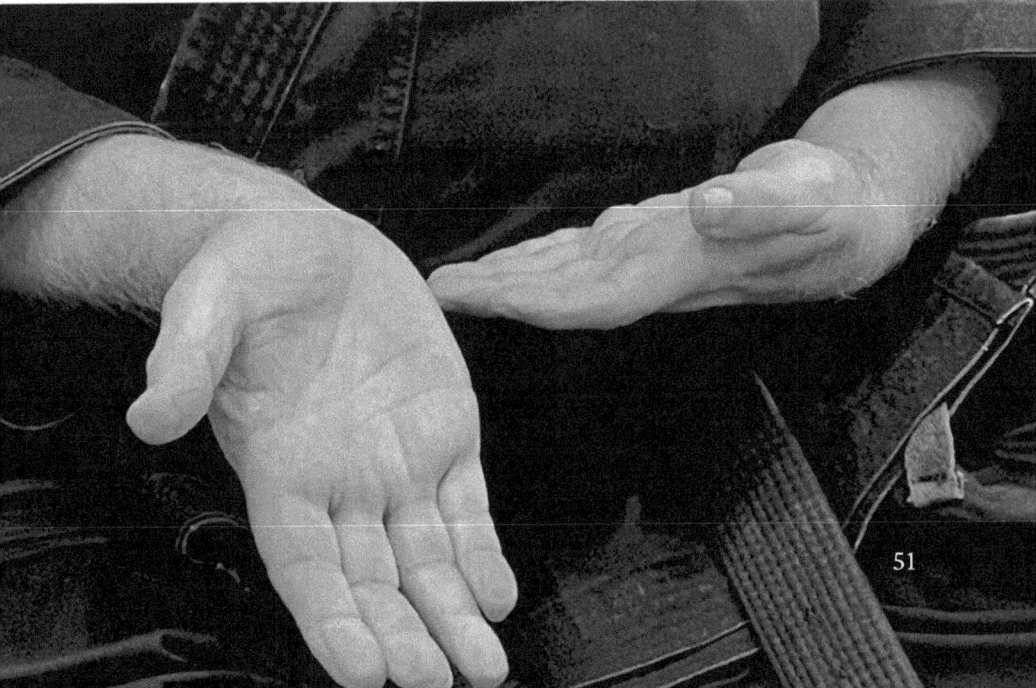

*Wisdom From the Ninja Village of the Cold Moon*

**A**mida Nyorai as personification of fire!

In the west
we behold the impact of highest self as
artist
expresser of significance
toucher of hearts
one who reaches outward for connection.

Each of us
in his or her own unique way
wants to be
acknowledged and appreciated.
We all long to be
*respected and loved.*

Affection
is energy, but...
Beware of the corruption that turns connection with all into
desperately grasping in all directions for others out of fear of lack.

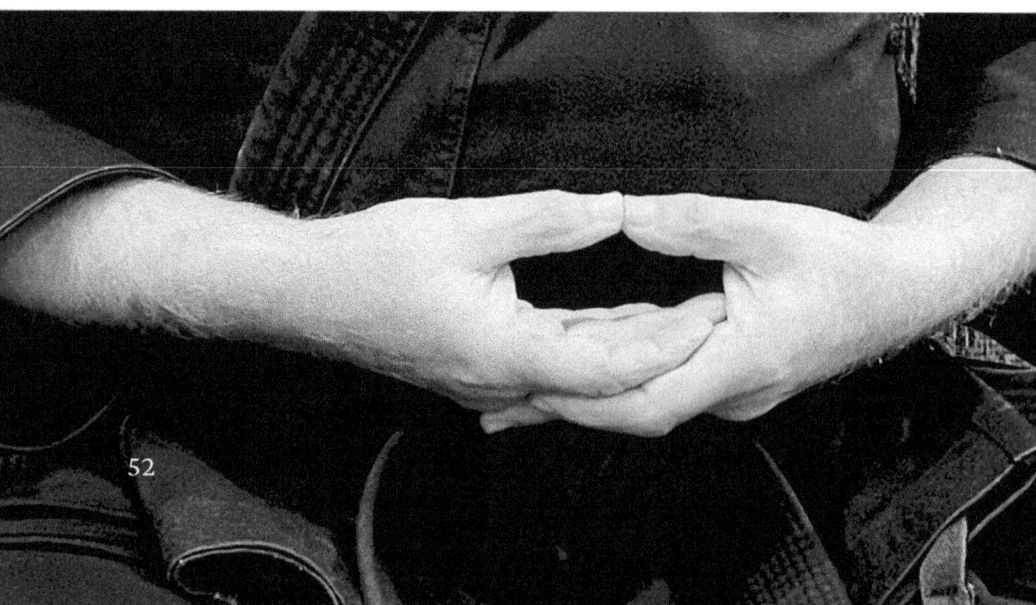

*Viewing Reality*

**F**ukujoju Nyorai as personification of wind!

In the north
we behold the stirring of highest self as
warrior
server
expander of the boundaries
one who transcends self for the sake of the ideal.

Each of us
in his or her own unique way
wants to be
part of something bigger than self.
We all long to serve something grand enough to be worthy of us.
We all wish to be *needed*.

Action
is freedom, but...
Beware of the corruption that turns efficient action into
competitive insecurity out of fear and envy of others' success.

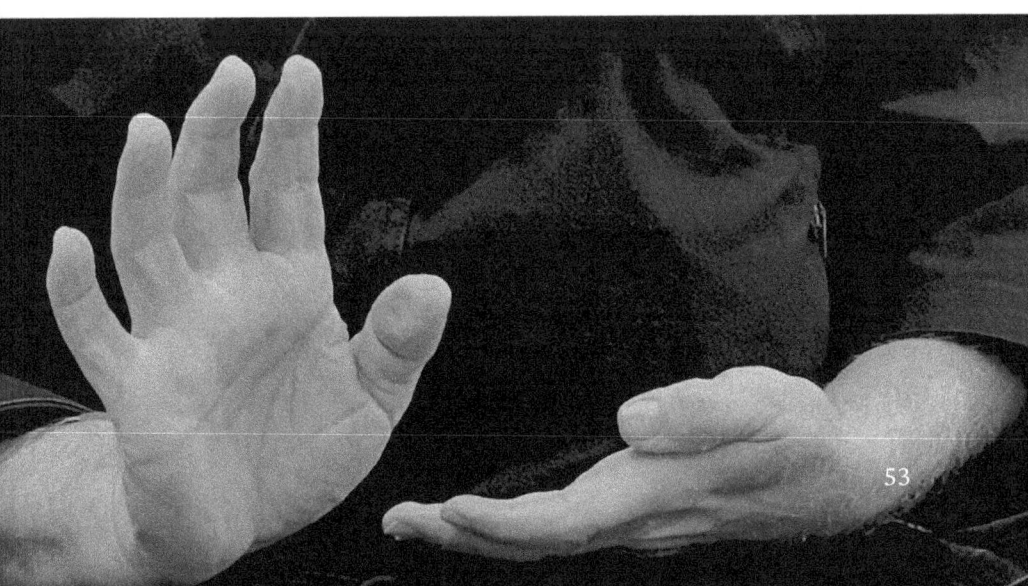

*Wisdom From the Ninja Village of the Cold Moon*

**D**ainichi Nyorai as personification of the void!

In the center
we behold the brilliance of highest self as
brightness
beholder of vast vision
actualizer of potential
one who holds all the inner keys to attainment.

Each of us
in his or her own unique way
wants to live up to
our own highest potential.
We all long to attain
the "exciting peace" of
*fulfillment and completion.*

Actualization
is fulfillment, but...
Beware of the corruption that turns grandest perception into
complacent thinking out of fear and confusion.

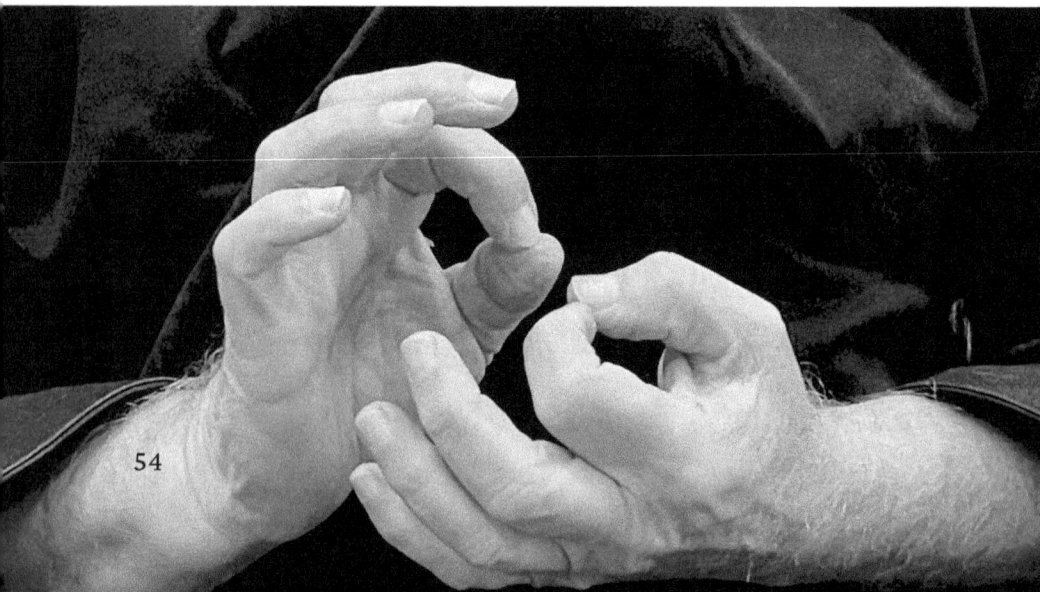

*Viewing Reality*

For the ninja,
being powerful
is the most loving thing
he can do.

*Wisdom From the Ninja Village of the Cold Moon*

In the words and actions
of the wise
there can arise
the appearance of contradiction.

Those aspiring to enlightenment
would be advised to hold in their hearts
the reassuring truth
that the inside of the universe is vast enough
to contain comfortably
all the paradoxes,
all the pieces of the puzzle
that we have not yet touched.

***Nin-po ik-kan***
  ***magokoro ni masare!***

"The ninja's consistent observation of
    the universal laws
        must take precedence
            over the dictates of the heart."

It is not our role
to explain intellectually
the vast fluctuations and permutations
of the cosmic scheme.

Painful though it may sometimes be
to our mortal sensitivities,
obscure though it may sometimes be
to the limits of our human vision,
we strive to embody and personify
the will and intention of the driving force
of all that must be.

This realization is the burden
and privilege
of the divine warrior.

# UNFOLDING
## OF THE ELEMENTS

*Wisdom From the Ninja Village of the Cold Moon*

**K**now that the heavens and earth were created
from a foundation of the five elements.
One piece
a small mirror of all others.
It is all the same.
All the same.

Each piece of existence
is its own small universe.
Earth
    Water
        Fire
            Air
And the potential of the great Emptiness
are there in everything.

To know the order of the universe
is to understand the ways of nature
and the proclivities of humankind.

*Wisdom From the Ninja Village of the Cold Moon*

**F**rom the rocks and earth
we learn of abundance, command, and stability.

When all about you is frantic chaos,
do not be absorbed by the crashing of gongs,
the screams of the hysterical,
or the wails of the grieving.

Lower your hips a bit.
Get closer to the earth.
Become one with the rocks
that never feel the need to weep.
Become a part of the plains
that never feel the need
to shift about at the whim of temporal happenings.
Your roots are buried deep
like those of the mountains.

When the inevitable events of life seem as though
they would sweep you away,
remember

You are the earth.

*Wisdom From the Ninja Village of the Cold Moon*

From the water
we learn of truth, science, and flexibility.

There will come times in your life
when you will find yourself quite alone
moving against vast armies
bearing swords
or contrary ideas.

Concentrate your spirit in the pit of your stomach
and be like the water.
The river rushes on ever alive
directed in its course by the very rocks
that it slowly
stealthily
wears away and destroys.
Be like the waves
impossible to grasp
and yet bafflingly strong in their fluidity.

There can be power in softness
victory in yielding.

When a clash with the tumultuous
would surely bring defeat,
remember

You are the water.

*Wisdom From the Ninja Village of the Cold Moon*

**F**rom the fire
we learn of connection, commitment, and intensity.

There are those who go through life
like so many moths.
Encountering breezes and bright windows in the night
as such things happen along.
Whimsically in mild confusion fluttering through days
until finally falling in foolish innocence
into the lantern's flame.

Allow energy to burst forth from beneath your ribs.
And be as the flame.
Direct your will.
The raw iron blade howls
when subjected to the intensity of the fire
and yet emerges from the forge with a purity
that promises immortality.
Be as the fire that is heat and light for others.
Provide confidence through your warmth
and inspiration through your enlightenment.

When caught in the dusty webs of those who would drain or
misdirect the energy of your being,
remember

You are the fire.

*Wisdom From the Ninja Village of the Cold Moon*

*Unfolding Of The Elements*

**F**rom the wind
we learn of freedom, service, and usefulness.

The allies of my grandfather
are now ominously silent behind fortress walls,
and last generation's enemy works beside us
building roadways through the mountains.

If only men would realize that
all fathers delight in the laughter of their daughters.
There is room in the sky
for the crow and cloud alike.

Feel your soul gather in your heart
and become attuned to the air.
Be like the wind
that plays with the gowns of the ladles of the court
and lifts the tattered kite of the fisherman's child
with the same gust.
Be like the air ever everywhere.
Purring through the throat of the sleeping house cat
and rustling the leaves in the mouse's den.

When others around you
lock into the rigid limitations born of egotism,
remember

You are the wind.

*Wisdom From the Ninja Village of the Cold Moon*

*Unfolding Of The Elements*

**F**rom the ethereal heavens
we learn to see and understand the big picture.

You are not locked in that body of yours.
Do not be afraid to explore
the dynamic potential of all things in the universe.
Quest ever on
to know,
feel,
and be
all that you possibly can.

Your singular essence sings from your throat
and joins the universal vibration of the heavens.
Become a part of the ethereal and look down upon the earth as it
plays its part in the cosmos.
Tap the knowledge of the heavens
to see the scheme of impersonal totality
and become a part
of the mind and eyes of the divine.

In the course of daily strife
that would lock you into the futility of
ignorance and delusion,
remember

You are the ethereal heavens.
You are capable of anything.

# HARMONY
## WITH THE
# COSMOS

The secret signs of the *kuji-in;*
hands entwined knowingly
in the patterns of intention
practiced to attain the mind and eyes
of the very gods themselves.

The mind directs
the energy of the physical entity
into harmony with the state of the universe.
The fingers interwoven
to channel the determination,
a tensing of the bones and muscles,
passage of the breath
and setting of the resolve
propel the ninja
to seize and ride the winds of fate.

*Wisdom From the Ninja Village of the Cold Moon*

**F**rom the grand and eternal oneness
existing from the aeons before existence
evolved the fundamental great polarity.
The one became the two
***in*** and ***yo***
the cosmic concepts of female and male.
From the two arose the potential of the ten thousand
in which is always reflected
the polarity of the two
and the affinity for returning to the one.
***Yo*** contains the sun.
***In***, the moon.
***Yo***, the heavens.
***In***, the earth.
***Yo***, the firm and bright.
***In***, the soft and dark.
The active ***yo***,
the passive ***in***,
as the polarities play out their games
of attraction and repulsion,
creation and destruction,
ever evolving
into one another.

**Ban-pen fu-kyo!**

"Ten thousand changes, no surprise!"

There is no surprise for the ninja.
Gain perspective
by expanding perceptions.
If everything is change
then reality is at best temporary.
Approach falsehood
as though it were truth
and truth
as though it were falsehood.
See the distant
as though it were near
and the close
as though it were far.
Make small decisions
as though they were crucial
and major choices
as though they were insignificant.

There are times when
strength is really a weakness,
laughter is power,
*in* is *yo*,
and innocence is wisdom.

*Wisdom From the Ninja Village of the Cold Moon*

**Shi-kin**

*Hara-mitsu*

***Dai-ko-myo!***

"The impact of this encounter
    could be key to ultimate breakthrough
        to a great bright awakening!"

This face
this voice
this touch
this aroma
this song
this fight
this embrace
this echo
now before you.
There!
Why do you falter?
Here is the answer
you have sought for a lifetime.
If only you could remember
asking the question.

*Harmony With The Cosmos*

Cutting the air with
the ghostly grid of power
from the land of eternal snows
five across
four down
the sacred nine slashes
of the warrior wizards of the night.

**Rin pyo toh sha kai jin retsu zai zen**

Seemingly summoning
the powers of the netherworld
  ...in truth, the strengths of our forefathers...
the nine ways of prevailing against all odds
in a manner consistent with
all that will be
all that ever was.

# CLOSE OF LIFE

*Close Of Life*

It is said that the warrior becomes invincible
by learning to live with his own death.
This is a misreading
of a great and important lesson.

Our death is with us ever-present
on our journey through life.

Death is not to be feared
but happily accepted
as a loving messenger who reminds us of
the priceless potential
of each of our todays.

There is a game you can play with death
in order to more fully know life.
Pretend that you have the knowledge
that you will meet your death
one week hence.
Use the pretended urgency
to give vitality to your hours.
Share all your secrets in your final days.
Express all your love.
Work through your desires.
Provide for those who will remain
when you are gone.

Carry out this pretense every day
and whether indeed you meet your death or not
you will have won a lifetime rich
in pleasure,
growth and wisdom,
and service.

*Wisdom From the Ninja Village of the Cold Moon*

In this manner
when the inevitability of death descends upon you
whether by way of the blade or the cold wind,
your body will be satisfied with memories of
warmth and meaning
and your spirit will be content
with the joy of its lessons.

You have been provided with a death
so that you may realize
the startling significance of why
you are here as a human being
and not as a cooking pot.

# ADMONITIONS
## OF THE
# KNOWING

*Admonitions Of The Knowing*

**B**eloved child!
This scroll of authority carries
the once-fresh ink and seal
of your grandfather's grandfather,
now but faded black and pale red.
The rest of this scroll offers
fresh open white space
as hint of what one future day will be
but faded ink and seal
from your aged hand
a hundred years ago.

*Wisdom From the Ninja Village of the Cold Moon*

**D**o not speak to us
of that which could have been.

All that was
is
all that could have been.

No more.

No less.

Let us level our gaze
and move purposefully into
today.

## Admonitions Of The Knowing

# ABOUT THE AUTHOR

From the apple cider autumn and college football world of his childhood home in Midwestern Ohio, Stephen K. Hayes began a lifelong odyssey that took him all the way around the world to the haunted, fog shrouded peaks and pine forests of the remote mountain regions of south central Japan. Seeking timeless secrets that would afford him mastery over his own life's progress and provide him guidance for creating a harmonious world around him, he gave up all that he had known and became an apprentice in the thousand-year-old tradition of Japan's *ninja* shadow warriors.

He was an experienced martial artist still seeking the ultimate contemporary combat method for what he then perceived as a hostile and competitive world. The heritage he found was that of warrior priests, consummate masters of resourcefulness, possessors of the secrets of generations of shadow warriors. He was led to discover a method for training for peace of spirit. He was initiated onto the path toward awakening through the cultivation of personal power. This was indeed the legacy that he had been born to pursue. This was the culture that had been destined to teach him.

He was trained in secret methods of silent movement and subtle combat techniques for protecting the gentle of the world. He was exposed to ways of altering his viewpoint to grasp a greater and truer scope of reality. He was prodded on to discover a deep self-knowledge that would allow him to work as a part of the universal scheme of totality.

After his years of apprenticeship, Stephen K. Hayes returned to his native North America with credentials as teacher in the Togakure ninja warrior lineage, and ordained practitioner in the esoteric *yamabushi* mountain seeker tradition of mind and spirit science.

Stephen K. Hayes was born in Wilmington, Delaware, in 1949, and grew up in Dayton, Ohio. He has traveled throughout North America, Europe, the Arctic, Japan, China, Tibet, Nepal, and India. A husband and grandfather, he is a writer, teacher, and ardent student of life.

A graduate of Miami University in Oxford, Ohio, Stephen K. Hayes majored in speech and theater. During his years in Japan, he used his professional acting talents in a variety of Japanese television and film projects. Most notable to American audiences was his role beside Richard Chamberlain in the NBC mini-series **Shogun**.

He is the author of a collection of books ranging from an album of poems and photographs to an international industrial espionage thriller to instructional texts on how to apply the timeless knowledge of the East in contemporary Western life. Several of his volumes have been published in a variety of different foreign languages as well.

Stephen K. Hayes began his formal training in the Asian martial arts as a teenager in the mid-1960s. By the autumn of 1985, he had earned a place in the prestigious Black Belt Hall of Fame, honoring him for his years of pioneering work introducing the Japanese ninja martial art to the American public. He was honored with a place in the Martial Arts History Museum in 2007, and was the sole winner of the Martial Arts Industry Association lifetime achievement award in 2015. Black Belt Magazine once referred to him as *"A legend; one of the ten most influential martial arts masters alive in the world today"*.

Throughout the 1990s and into the 2000s, he served as personal protection agent and security advisor for the Dalai Lama of Tibet, 1989 winner of the Nobel Peace Prize.

In the early 1990s, he was part of a secret United States defensive initiative known as Project Stargate, where he used psychic remote viewing skills to decipher distant enemy locations.

He is the founder of the martial art of To-Shin Do, a mind and body self-protection system based on the ancient ninja martial arts principles updated for application to modern threats and pressures.

Stephen K. Hayes' and his wife Rumiko oversee training dedicated to the sciences of self-development. He travels the world as a teacher, seminar leader, and lecturer. His informative and inspiring presentations translate his extensive background in the martial and meditation arts into practical lessons for handling the pressures, choices, uncertainties, and stresses of life in the modern western world.

Stephen K. Hayes' interpretation of Japan's ancient warrior path of enlightenment creates a basis for understanding the power of directed intention as a tool for accomplishment in all areas of life. He emphasizes to audiences around the world:

"Personal success, whether it be in the realms of physical, intellectual, economic, or spiritual breakthroughs, begins with paying attention to the awakening of potential. We cultivate a state of fearlessness and resolve in recognition of the reality that there will be times when things do not go the way we want. We can learn to live positively and generate the results we need in life by creating a *momentum of accomplishment*. Our training program shows us how to begin. It is then up to our own resourcefulness and commitment as to how far we take ourselves."

For information on the disciplines taught by Stephen K. Hayes, contact:
SKH Quest
PO Box 326
Bellbrook, OH 45370 USA

www.StephenKHayes.com

www.ingramcontent.com/pod-product-compliance
Lightning Source LLC
Chambersburg PA
CBHW051615010526
44107CB00037B/1438/J